MEXICO
BEAUTIFUL LAND
DIVERSE PEOPLE

THE STATES OF NORTHERN MEXICO

DEIRDRE DAY-MACLEOD

UNITED STATES

108°W   106°W   104°W   102°W

100°W   98°W

32°N

Ciudad Juárez

CHIHUAHUA

30°N

Chihuahua

28°N

COAHUILA

N
W   E
S

Nuevo
Laredo

26°N

MEXICO

NUEVO
LEÓN

Reynosa
Matamoros

Torreón

Saltillo

Monterrey

DURANGO

24°N

Durango

ZACATECAS

Ciudad
Victoria

TAMAULIPAS

PACIFIC
OCEAN

Zacatecas

Gulf of Mexico

SAN LUIS
POTOSÍ

22°N

San Luis Potosí

0   100   200 Miles

0   100   200 Kilometers
Albers Conic Equal-Area Projection

MEXICO
BEAUTIFUL LAND
DIVERSE PEOPLE

THE STATES OF NORTHERN MEXICO

DIERDRE DAY-MACLEOD

Mason Crest Publishers

Philadelphia

Mason Crest Publishers
370 Reed Road
Broomall PA 19008
www.masoncrest.com

First printing

1 3 5 7 9 8 6 4 2

Library of Congress Cataloging-in-Publication Data on file at the Library of Congress

Day-MacLeod, Deirdre.
  The states of northern Mexico / Deirdre Day MacLeod.
      p. cm. — (Mexico—beautiful land, diverse people)
  Includes index.
  ISBN 978-1-4222-0665-2 (hardcover) — ISBN 978-1-4222-0732-1 (pbk.)
  1. Mexico, North—Juvenile literature. I. Title.
  F1314.D38 2008
  972—dc22
                                                    2008031852

TABLE OF CONTENTS

MEXICO
BEAUTIFUL LAND
DIVERSE PEOPLE

THE ECONOMY OF MEXICO

FAMOUS PEOPLE OF MEXICO

THE FESTIVALS OF MEXICO

THE FOOD OF MEXICO

THE GEOGRAPHY OF MEXICO

THE GOVERNMENT OF MEXICO

THE HISTORY OF MEXICO

MEXICAN ART AND ARCHITECTURE

THE PEOPLE OF MEXICO

SPORTS OF MEXICO

THE GULF STATES OF MEXICO

THE STATES OF NORTHERN MEXICO

THE PACIFIC SOUTH STATES OF MEXICO

THE STATES OF CENTRAL MEXICO

THE PACIFIC NORTH STATES OF MEXICO

MEXICO: FACTS AND FIGURES

INTRODUCTION

exico is a country in the midst of great change. And what happens in Mexico reverberates in the United States, its neighbor to the north.

For outsiders, the most obvious of Mexico's recent changes has occurred in the political realm. From 1929 until the end of the 20th century, the country was ruled by a single political party: the Partido Revolucionario Institucional, or PRI (in English, the Institutional Revolutionary Party). Over the years, PRI governments became notorious for corruption, and the Mexican economy languished. In 2000, however, the PRI's stranglehold on national politics was broken with the election of Vicente Fox as Mexico's president. Fox, of the Partido de Acción Nacional (National Action Party), or PAN, promised political reform and economic development but had a mixed record as president. However, another PAN candidate, Felipe Calderón, succeeded Fox in 2006 after a hotly contested and highly controversial election. That election saw Calderón win by the slimmest of margins over a candidate from the Partido de la Revolución Democrática (Party of the Democratic Revolution). The days of one-party rule in Mexico, it seems, are gone for good.

Mexico's economy, like its politics, has seen significant changes in recent years. A 1994 free-trade agreement with the United States and Canada, along with the increasing transfer of industries from government control to private ownership under President Fox and President Calderón, has helped spur economic growth in Mexico. When all the world's countries are compared,

Mexico now falls into the upper-middle range in per-capita income. This means that, on average, Mexicans enjoy a higher standard of living than people in the majority of the world's countries. Yet averages can be misleading. In Mexico there is an enormous gap between haves and have-nots. According to some estimates, 40 percent of the country's more than 100 million people live in poverty. In some areas of Mexico, particularly in rural villages, jobs are almost nonexistent. This has driven millions of Mexicans to immigrate to the United States (with or without proper documentation) in search of a better life.

By 2006 more than 11 million people born in Mexico were living in the United States (including more than 6 million illegal immigrants), according to estimates based on data from the Pew Hispanic Center and the U.S. Census Bureau. Meanwhile, nearly one of every 10 people living in the United States was of Mexican ancestry. Clearly, Mexico and Mexicans have had—and will continue to have—a major influence on American society.

It is especially unfortunate, then, that many American students know little about their country's neighbor to the south. The books in the MEXICO: BEAUTIFUL LAND, DIVERSE PEOPLE series are designed to help correct that.

As readers will discover, Mexico boasts a rich, vibrant culture that is a blend of indigenous and European—especially Spanish—influences. More than 3,000 years ago, the Olmec people created a complex society and built imposing monuments that survive to this day in the Mexican states of Tabasco and Veracruz. In the fifth century A.D., when the Roman Empire collapsed and Europe entered its so-called Dark Age, the Mayan civilization was already flourishing in the jungles of the Yucatán Peninsula—and it would enjoy another four centuries of tremendous cultural achievements. By the time the Spanish conqueror Hernán Cortés landed at Veracruz in 1519, another great indigenous civilization, the Aztecs, had emerged to dominate much of Mexico.

With a force of about 500 soldiers, plus a few horses and cannons, Cortés marched inland toward the Aztec capital, Tenochtitlán. Built in the middle of a lake in what is now Mexico City, Tenochtitlán was an engineering marvel and one of the largest cities anywhere in the world at the time. With allies from among the indigenous peoples who resented being ruled by the Aztecs—and aided by a smallpox epidemic—Cortés and the Spaniards managed to conquer the Aztec Empire in 1521 after a brutal fight that devastated Tenochtitlán.

It was in that destruction that modern Mexico was born. Spaniards married indigenous people, creating mestizo offspring—as well as a distinctive Mexican culture that was neither Spanish nor indigenous but combined elements of both.

Spain ruled Mexico for three centuries. After an unsuccessful revolution in 1810, Mexico finally won its independence in 1821.

But the newly born country continued to face many difficulties. Among them were bad rulers, beginning with a military officer named Agustín Iturbide, who had himself crowned emperor only a year after Mexico threw off the yoke of Spain. In 1848 Mexico lost a war with the United States—and was forced to give up almost half of its territory as a result. During the 1860s French forces invaded Mexico and installed a puppet emperor. While Mexico regained its independence in 1867 under national hero Benito Juárez, the long dictatorship of Porfirio Díaz would soon follow.

Díaz was overthrown in a revolution that began in 1910, but Mexico would be racked by fighting until the Partido Revolucionario Institucional took over in 1929. The PRI brought stability and economic progress, but its rule became increasingly corrupt.

Today, with the PRI's long monopoly on power swept away, Mexico stands on the brink of a new era. Difficult problems such as entrenched inequalities and grinding poverty remain. But progress toward a more open political system may lead to economic and social progress as well. Mexico—a land with a rich and ancient heritage—may emerge as one of the 21st century's most inspiring success stories.

An old church is tucked into a canyon in the Sierra Madre Mountains of Chihuahua. Many of Mexico's colonial buildings remain standing throughout the country.

THE LAND

Imagine Mexico as a giant letter "vee" with its the top opening toward the United States. Two rugged mountain ranges form the edges of the vee—the "Mother" mountains: the Sierra Madre Oriental and the Sierra Madre Occidental. In the north, they are wide apart, separated by the *Meseta Central* (the Central **Plateau**). The northern states of Mexico lie within the top of this vee. This region is composed of seven states: Chihuahua, Coahuila, Durango, Nuevo León, San Luis Potosí, Tamaulipas, and Zacatecas.

When you look at a map of Mexico it is difficult to tell which areas are *tierra caliente, tierra templada,* or *tierra fría*—the hot-, medium-, and cold-weather areas. This is because the climate in Mexico is determined not by whether the land is in the north or the south as much as by elevation—the higher up in the mountains, the cooler the region. Much of this area falls into the medium-weather or temperate zone. The state of Tamaulipas, which lies along the Gulf Coast, however, is *tierra caliente,* as is the northernmost part of the land that slopes down toward the Río Grande.

The northern edge of this area lies along the Río Grande, the 2,000-mile border river shared with the United States. The Río Grande, called the Río Bravo by the Mexicans, is a shallow winding river that empties into the Gulf of Mexico. It brings together rivers from all along the eastern side of Mexico.

The Chihuahua Desert lies just south of the Río Grande. In the native language, Chihuahua means "dry, sandy land," and the Chihuahua is the largest desert in North America. This desert covers about 175,000 square miles and is bigger than the entire state of California. It is called a "rain shadow desert," because the two mountain ranges on either side of it stop the moist air from the Gulf of Mexico and the Pacific Ocean from reaching the middle area. Unlike many deserts, the Chihuahua is not flat. There are many small mountain ranges running through it, and within the cracks between mountains are river basins. The differences in altitude mean that the Chihuahua is home to more kinds of wildlife than most other deserts.

The Indians who once inhabited this area could not farm but lived by hunting and gathering, sometimes eating the cactus or even iguanas and insects. There are 500 different kinds of cactus in Mexico, and Indians once used some of them for food and drink. The dry land cannot support much life unless it is *irrigated*.

Deep canyons cut through this rough scenery. The flat area, called "Meseta Central"—the central plateau—is cradled between the two jagged mountain ranges. The land sloping toward the Río Grande has become a region of large cities with sky scrapers and factories. It is also a land where there are still Indians living in caves. Orchards and

This vibrantly striped kingsnake can be found in the mountains of Durango. The range of climates of Mexico create comfortable habitats for a unique variety of animals, reptiles, and birds.

croplands flourish in fertile valleys reclaimed by irrigation.

The area known as Copper Canyon is twice the size of the Grand Canyon in Arizona. Copper Canyon is not a single canyon but the union of several deep, spectacular canyons. It is cut by the Urique River and has deep, wide gorges so remote that parts of it have never been explored on foot. This region is also known as the Sierra Tarahumara, after the Indians who live there. No copper is found here; the canyon is named for the color of its walls.

The Sierra Madre Occidental forms the western rim of the Plateau of Mexico, and it runs from Chihuahua down through Durango and then into Zacatecas, the Mexican states that lie to the south. For hundreds of years, this mountain range blocked transportation between the plateau and the west coast, forming a natural barrier. Paved roads and a railroad were not built across it until the 1900s.

The Chihuahua Desert stretches across several Mexican states, as well as across the border and into the United States. This fishhook barrel cactus thrives in Nuevo León.

This range includes some of Mexico's most rugged land. Short, steep streams flowing to the Pacific Ocean have cut canyons more than a mile (1.6 kilometers) deep through the mountains.

Higher in the mountains, the weather gets colder. Here bear and sheep live. In the winter the forests at the tops of the mountains may be covered in snow, while the valleys beneath are still tropically warm. These western mountains climb to the height of 9,200 feet. The Tarahumara Indians *migrate* from the caves where they live in the summer, down to the warmer areas when frigid winter winds arrive. The state of Durango is also famous for its huge desert scorpions.

The Sierra Madre Oriental, the plateau's eastern rim, runs through the states of Coahuila and Nuevo León. These mountains are actually a series of ranges. In many places, between the ranges, highways and railroads climb up to the plateau from the east coast. Though

These Tarahumara Indian girls are wearing traditional dresses. The Tarahumara are descended from natives of Mexico. Most live in the Sierra Madre Mountains apart from Mexico's mestizo civilization.

the Sierra Madre Oriental is not a region of abundance agriculturally, this area is rich in metals such as silver, gold, lead, iron, and zinc.

In Tamaulipas, beside the Gulf of Mexico, the land is flat and low with marshes and lagoons, alligators and crocodiles. This is *tierra caliente* or hot land. Tamaulipas borders the United States on the north, Veracruz and San Luis Potosí to the south, Veracruz and the Gulf of Mexico to the east. In the native people's language, the name may mean "High Mountains," "Tribe of Olives," or "Place of Much Prayer." In the north, Tamaulipas is fairly dry and warm with only a little rain. In the south and southeast it is warmer and wetter. In the mountains, the climate ranges from warm to temperate according to altitude.

There are places in Tamaulipas so remote that the people who live there don't use money. Many of these live in a protected region called

Intricate and elaborate sculpture surrounds the altarpiece in a side chapel of the Templo de Carmen in San Luis Potosí. The Roman Catholic religion dominates Mexico, with over three-fourths of the population members of the church.

the "El Cielo" biosphere reserve. This is an area where all the wildlife and plants are protected from harm.

The Huasteca is the region of the Sierra Madre Oriental that covers the south of Tamaulipas as well as the northern region of San Luis Potosí (and Veracruz). It rains there between 60 and 150 inches annually. Much of the Huasteca is covered with tropical cloud forests. Here you can find spectacular waterfalls, cenotes (sinkholes), and lush canyons that are an amazing contrast to the high dry deserts just a few hours away.

CHIHUAHUA

Location: Sonora lies to the west; Coahuila to the east; the United States to the north; and Durango to the south.

Capital: Chihuahua

Total area: 96,364 square miles (247,087 sq km)

Climate: Mostly dry and warm; colder at higher elevations

Terrain: Desert, canyons, some forests at higher elevations

Elevation: High 10,725 feet (3,250 meters) Low 4,921 feet (1,500 meters)

Natural hazards: Drought, earthquakes

COAHUILA

Location: The United States lies to the north; Nuevo León to the east; San Luis Potosí and Zacatecas to the south; and Durango and Chihuahua to the northeast.

Capital: Saltillo

Total area: 58,493 square miles (149,982 sq km)

Climate: Mild, dry

Terrain: Deserts and mountains

Elevation: High 12,172 feet (3,700 meters) Low 2,625 feet (800 meters)

Natural hazards: Earthquakes

DURANGO

Location: Chihuahua and Coahuila lie to the north; Zacatecas to the east; Nayarit to the south; and Sinaloa to the west.

Capital: Durango

Total area: 46,663 square miles (119,648 sq km)

Climate: Moderate with four seasons

Terrain: Mountainous

Elevation: High 10,956 feet (3,320 meters) Low

Natural hazards: Earthquakes

17

NUEVO LEÓN

Location: Surrounded by Coahuila to the west and north; Tamaulipas to the east; San Luis Potosí and Zacatecas to the south.

Capital: Monterrey

Total area:
25,176 square miles
(64,555 sq km)

Climate: Hot, humid

Terrain: Mountainous

Elevation: High 12,139 feet (3,700 meters) Low 2,953 feet
(900 meters)

Natural hazards:
Earthquakes, mud slides

SAN LUIS POTOSÍ

Location: Coahuila lies to the south, Nuevo León and Tamaulipas to the northeast; Veracruz to the east; Guanajuato, Querétaro, and Hidalgo to the south; and Zacatecas to the west.

Capital: San Luis Potosí

Total area:
24,511 square miles
(62,848 sq km)

Climate: Tropical to cool and arid, depending on altitude.

Terrain: Mountainous

Elevation: High 9,843 feet (3,000 meters) Low 223 feet
(68 meters)

Natural hazards:
Earthquakes

TAMAULIPAS

Location: The United States lies to the north; Veracruz and San Luis Potosí are to the south; the Gulf of Mexico is to the east; and Nuevo León is to the west.

Capital: Ciudad Victoria

Total area: 31,133 square miles (79,829 sq km)

Climate: The north-central part is semi-dry and semi-warm, with scarce rain. The south and southeast parts are warm, with summer rains.

Terrain: Mountainous away from the coast

Elevation: High 9,843 feet (3,000 meters) Low Sea level

Natural hazards: Hurricanes

ZACATECAS

Location: Durango lies to the northwest; Coahuila to the northeast; San Luis Potosí to the east; and Jalisco and Aguascalientes to the south.

Capital: Zacatecas

Total area: 58,654 square miles (150,395 sq km)

Climate: Four types of climate, depending on altitude: semi-warm, dry, mild, and cold.

Terrain: Mountainous

Elevation: High 10,499 feet (3,200 meters) Low 6,594 feet (2,010 meters)

Natural hazards: Earthquakes, volcanoes

The Metropolitan Cathedral of Our Lady of Monterrey looms over Monterrey, Nuevo León. The cathedral's architecture blends a variety of styles, reflecting the diverse influences of northern Mexico's history.

THE HISTORY

The stories that have come to us about the history of the northern parts of Mexico are as beautiful and as brutal as the land itself. Long ago, tribes called Chichimecas lived in these desert regions. They could not grow food in land that had no water, nor could they raise livestock. They wandered from place to place, wintering in the warmer parts and spending their summers up higher in the mountains. They would eat whatever they could find—snakes, reptiles, cactus, even insects. In the mountains, they could catch rabbits or gather wild foods.

These Chichimecas—the name given to all of the northern nomads regardless of their tribe—came down from northern Mexico to settle in the central region—the meseta—where the land was fertile and more forgiving. The word "Chichimeca" meant "lineage of the dog," but it was not meant as an insult. Rather, many Aztec dynasties were proud to claim this heritage. But while the Aztecs swept across central Mexico, conquering the other tribes, the people who remained in the north continued to live as they had. Some, such as the Tarahumara or *Rarámuri*, live in this fashion even today.

When the Spanish arrived, conquering the northern part of Mexico took them much longer than they had needed to control the central region of Mexico. For generations, roving tribes would come down from the mountains, attack the Spanish, and then retreat. The Spanish settlers who were brave enough to venture into northern Mexico were not *conquistadors* seeking treasure and fame. Instead, these were people who planned to stay—miners and ranchers and Catholic priests.

Between A.D. 1000 and 1200, the ancient city of Paquimé thrived in the area that today is the state of Chihuahua. It was the most important trading and farming center in northern Mexico. The people who lived there kept parrots and turkeys in pens; they built *aqueducts* and *cisterns* to supply their city with fresh water. By the time the Spanish came to Mexico, however, the people of Paquimé had disappeared, and the Aztecs had burned their abandoned buildings. Archeologists did not discover the long-ago city until the 1970s.

When the Spanish came to this land, they brought with them horses, cattle, and sheep—and the desert became ranchland that at one time stretched beyond the Río Grande into what is now the United States. The new animals from Europe altered the landscape. It became rangeland, where vast *haciendas* stretched for miles and miles. In Chihuahua, *vaqueros* originated the riding and roping skills we now associate with American cowboys.

The land was secluded and wild, separated from civilization by the desert's sandstorms. During the Mexican Revolution, this seclusion appealed to Pancho Villa, the rebel leader. He established his headquarters in Chihuahua; his band of cowboys and bandits streamed out of the

This mural depicts aspects of ancient Aztec life. Many theorize that the Aztecs migrated from northern Mexico in the early 13th century.

desert to attack the unjust government of Porfirio Díaz—and then they retreated back to the safety of the desert.

COAHUILA

The state of Coahuila is proud of the part it played in Mexican history. Two great leaders of the nation's fight for freedom and equal rights were born in Saltillo, the state's capital city. The first of these, Francisco Madero, was the first political leader to seize power from Porfirio Díaz, whose harsh rule controlled Mexico for more than 30 years. Madero, a wealthy landowner, challenged Díaz in the elections, and as a result Madero was imprisoned. After his release, Madero fled to the United States, where he called for revolution in Mexico. Under his leadership, the

One of the most influential revolutionaries of his time, Francisco "Pancho" Villa was considered a champion of the Mexican Revolution in the early 20th century.

Mexican Revolution was launched, and Díaz was overthrown.

The second revolutionary leader to come from Coahuila was Venustiano Carranza. He was a military general who is called the

"Father of the Mexican Constitution." He became the governor of his state, and then went on to become the nation's president.

DURANGO

When the Spanish began to settle northern Mexico, their coming nearly destroyed the native people who already lived there. The Spanish turned the Indians into slaves; many of the native people died because they had no *immunities* to the diseases the Spanish brought with them; and the Spanish missionaries tried to take away the Indians' religion and replace it with Christianity.

Francisco Indalécio Madero was a Mexican revolutionary and politician. He opposed President Díaz and took over the presidency for two years, until his reign was overthown.

But some of the native people fought back. In Durango, between 1616 and 1620, the Tepehuán people fought for their freedom and their rights. The rebellion was led by a man named Quautlatas, who had been flogged by the *Jesuit* missionaries for expressing his doubts about Christianity. Quautlatas encouraged his people to reject Christianity, to recover their faith in their old beliefs, and to drive the

Spanish invaders out of their land. He traveled from settlement, fanning the fires of rebellion. He told his listeners that if they were killed in battle against the Spanish, they would be brought back to life seven days after their final victory.

The rebels burned churches and killed more than 400 Spanish settlers and missionaries. The Spanish responded by sending their troops to kill and defeat the Tepehuanes. More than a thousand of the native people were killed, and hundreds more were sold into slavery.

ZACATECAS

Durango was not the only region to experience Indian rebellion. In 1541, Indians in the area that is now Zacatecas burned down the churches and killed the owners of the haciendas. The Spanish swiftly and brutally squashed the uprising, forcing the Indians to flee into the highlands of Zacatecas, a land of steep hills and poisonous scorpions.

After this war, known as the Mixton War, the Spanish felt that they must overpower all the Indians. From Zacatecas, the Spanish moved to conquer the whole area of north-central Mexico. As mines flourished and farms were established, more and more Indians were either made into slaves or forced farther north to less desirable land.

NUEVO LEÓN

When the Spanish conquered this region they gave it the name of Nuevo Reino de León in honor of Reino de León, an area in Spain. In September 20, 1596, Don Diego de Montemayor, a Spanish conquistador, settled a city here with 12 families. At that time, the city was called La Villa de San Luis de Francia (named for the king of France), but Don Diego later changed the name to Ciudad Metropolitana de Nuestra Señora de Monterrey. Four hundred years later, Monterrey is a modern and industrial city, the third largest in Mexico.

SAN LUIS POTOSÍ

This region was first settled in 1583 as a Franciscan mission, but the community forgot its preoccupation with religion when someone discovered silver in the mountains. Because of the royal fortune beneath the land, it was given a new, royal name in 1592—San Luis, after King Louis IX of France. Potosí was the name of a rich Bolivian mining town, and this was tacked on as well, in hopes that this region would prove to be as prosperous as the Bolivian town.

By the 19th century, however, San Luis Potosí had become an out-of-the-way refuge for political liberals who were seeking to escape government persecution. After Napoléon's troops captured Mexico City in 1863, President Juárez brought the remains of his government to San Luis—but then he moved still further north, into Chihuahua.

At the time of the Mexican Revolution, San Luis was still a haven for liberal opposition to the government. Francisco Madero fled here after Díaz arrested him for challenging his presidency. Madero moved on across the border to San Antonio, Texas, but when he drafted his famous plan for a new government, he called it the *Plan de San Luis Potosí*. Madero managed to win his fight against Díaz, but he did not hold the presidency long. By 1913 he had been assassinated, and the revolution splintered in many warring factions.

On December 1, 2006, Felipe Calderón was sworn in as president of Mexico until 2012. Like his predecessor, Vicente Fox, Calderón is a member of the National Action Party (PAN), a party that leans conservative. As president, Calderón has addressed the problems of crime and poverty.

TAMAULIPAS

During the 1830s, the people of Tamaulipas opposed the central government's rule. They felt that the Mexican government was only plunging them into deeper and deeper economic trouble. They supported a *petition* that asked that the president get rid of the existing *cabinet*, and create an entirely new government.

At the time, Tamaulipas, Coahuila, Nuevo León, and Texas were a single military jurisdiction. Texas eventually achieved its independence from the Mexican government, but Tamaulipas, along with Coahuila and Nuevo León, remained under the Mexican government's repressive control until the Revolution of 1910 brought the entire nation greater freedom.

ZACATECAS

In the mid-16th century, a native Cascane from this region gave a silver trinket to one of the early Spanish colonists. The silver, the Cascane said, had come from the mountains of this land. The small gift sparked the mining rush that continued for the next two centuries. During these years more than a billion dollars worth of silver and other precious metals were stripped from the hills of Zacatecas.

By the 20th century, the mines were running dry, but Zacatecas still had an important part to play in Mexican history. The rebel leader Pancho Villa fought an important battle here during the Mexican Revolution, defeating the government's troops.

Northern Mexico may be a harsh and isolated land—but Mexico would not be the nation it is today without the part the northern states played in its history. After centuries of internal strife, Mexico held its first fair presidential election in decades, removing the controlling party from office with a peaceful transition of power in 2000. As president, Vicente Fox vowed to do all he could to heal the wounds of his country's troubled past. The election of Felipe Calderón in 2006, though disputed at first, suggests that peaceful and democratic elections will continue in Mexico as the nation develops.

A farmer stands among the dry stalks of corn in his field. In recent years, Mexico has been plagued by repeated droughts, making farming a particularly difficult way to make a living.

THE ECONOMY

Mexico has a long history of serious economic problems. The gap between the rich and the poor has been wide and deep, and the government has often done very little to solve the problems of a desperately poor population. Instead, year after year, the nation's economy grew weaker and weaker, while the government made a series of foolish decisions.

Today, however, Mexico is struggling to heal some of the many problems that have scarred its economy. The North American Free Trade Agreement (NAFTA) is one of the key factors in the economic growth of Mexico. This is especially true of the northern states that are so close to the U.S.–Mexican border.

NAFTA was negotiated between the United States, Mexico, and Canada in 1991, it was completed in 1993, and it became active on January 1, 1994. One goal of NAFTA is to remove trade restrictions between the countries over a 15-year time period. Import duties are abolished between participating countries. This means a country does not have to pay a tax to sell products from one country to another. The agreement brings Mexico into one of the largest trade zones in the world. NAFTA removes barriers and therefore speeds up the process of buying and selling. It provides more opportunities for investment and encourages cooperation between nations.

NAFTA is not the answer to all of the economic growth in Mexico, however. In some instances, in fact, it has created problems. In 1995, under President Zedillo, there was a financial crisis from an imbalance in trade. More was going out of the country than was coming in. *Interest rates* went up and people were having a hard time paying for necessary items. By 1999, however, Mexico's economic situation had begun to improve.

Maquiladoras have created much of the growth. The *maquiladoras* are assembly plants where the pieces of a product are **imported** into Mexico without any tax. The product is assembled in Mexico. It is then **exported** from Mexico, again without paying a tax. U.S. businesses are attracted to Mexican *maquiladoras* because they do not have to obey American safety regulations or pay their workers as much as they would have to in the United States; this means the factory owners can make their products more cheaply and sell them at a greater profit. Around the world, many people are concerned about the poor working conditions in Mexican *maquiladoras*.

However, despite the poor working conditions, and even though most of these plants or factories are owned by foreigners, they still boost the economy by providing jobs. This creates the need for more technology. More electricity, running water, housing, roads, and transportation are needed to support all of the people who are working in the *maquiladoras*.

A train runs along the Copper Canyon in the Sierra Madre Mountains. Mexico's tumultuous history and limited finances have brought about few improvements in its infrastructure and technology.

Nuevo León is is one of Mexico's leading industrial areas. It is easy to pass across a new international bridge to the United States, and there are numerous factories that produce iron and steel, glass, textiles, and petrochemicals. Monterrey is the financial center; the city's dozens of *maquiladoras* employ thousands of workers. Forty percent of the jobs in this state involve manufacturing. In fact, Nuevo León is one of the few places in Mexico where unemployment is not a problem. The government is working to train people to work in the factories because of a shortage of skilled labor.

However, due to the extreme heat and dryness, not much grows in Nuevo León. Cattle raising is the primary agricultural activity.

Silver purses hang for sale at a tourist market. Mexico's folk art is appreciated both inside and outside its borders. Tourism and the souvenir business are thriving.

Good railroads and highways in San Luis Potosí make transporting goods easy. Agriculture and cattle also play an important role in San Luis Potosí's economy. Most of the industry concerns automobiles, mining, food processing, mechanics, textiles, and beverage production. Although San Luis Potosí began as a mining settlement, today most of its economy is built around exporting goods.

The economy of Zacatecas depends mainly on agriculture, livestock, and mining. Main products include guavas, grapes, peaches, and apples. Cattle and sheep graze on more than half the land. Mining of silver, tin, lead, copper, and gold continues. Most of Mexico's silver comes from Zacatecas.

A young Tarahumara boy stands in a field. Farming is an essential part of Mexico's economy, and it provides the necessities for the family who must work the land.

Durango's economic strength is mining and forestry. More than a third of Mexico's timber comes from this state. Wood-related industries make paper, plywood, cross ties, and other wooden items. Most of the industry is located in Ciudad Lerdo and in Gómez Palacio. One third of Durango's economy is based on the farming of crops and livestock.

In Tamaulipas, agriculture is important. Efficient irrigation allows farmers to grow sorghum, wheat, and corn. Fishing along the coast depends upon shrimp, crayfish, oyster, and crabs. Oil production and maquiladoras account for most of the industry. The port of Tampico is one of the most active in the area.

**Hand-made bricks dry in the yard of a brick factory near Durango.
Manufacturing and industry have become key to Mexico's financial future.**

Coahuila gets most of its income from mining and industry.
Excellent highways allow goods to be transported easily. Fluorite, lead,
and tin mining are important to this state's economy. Foundries take
the raw materials and make steel and iron. Irrigation allows for
farming and livestock raising. The area of Laguna is one of Mexico's
richest farming regions.

Chihuahua, Mexico's largest state, depends on mining and industry
for 36 percent of its economy. Most of the manufacturing occurs in

maquiladoras along the U.S. border, in the two large cities, Ciudad Juárez and Chihuahua City. Ciudad Juárez remains the major manufacturing area, with about 400 factories in the same town that was at one time a stopping place for cowboys from El Paso. At the beginning of the last century, Chihuahua's economy was more concerned with timber and livestock, but today companies such as Toshiba, JRC, and Honeywell have factories here. In addition, Chihuahua has a number of tourist attractions, including the Copper Canyon.

Although there is no copper in Copper Canyon, the Spanish did find gold and silver as well as turquoise and amethyst there. Today many of the precious metals are gone, but a few prospectors are still trying to make a living there.

The Indians farm along the rivers, primarily raising corn. Almost every family tends to one milpa or cornfield, and there are six types of corn commonly grown here. Other important crops are beans, squash, peaches, apples, and potatoes.

maquiladoras along the U.S. border, in the two large cities, Ciudad Juárez and Chihuahua City. Ciudad Juárez remains the major manufacturing area, with about 400 factories in the same town that was at one time a stopping place for cowboys from El Paso. At the beginning of the last century, Chihuahua's economy was more concerned with timber and livestock, but today companies such as Toshiba, JRC, and Honeywell have factories here. In addition, Chihuahua has a number of tourist attractions, including the Copper Canyon.

Although there is no copper in Copper Canyon, the Spanish did find gold and silver as well as turquoise and amethyst there. Today many of the precious metals are gone, but a few prospectors are still trying to make a living there.

The Indians farm along the rivers, primarily raising corn. Almost every family tends to one milpa or cornfield, and there are six types of corn commonly grown here. Other important crops are beans, squash, peaches, apples, and potatoes.

CHIHUAHUA

GDP in thousands of pesos:
183,624,001
Percent of GDP:
Manufacturing: 11 percent
Commerce: 52 percent
Service industries: 37 percent
Per capita income in pesos: 19,817
Exports: Minerals, corn, wheat, beans, and meat.
Natural resources: timber, livestock

DURANGO

GDP in thousands of pesos:
52,542,937
Percent of GDP:
Manufacturing: 13 percent
Commerce: 53 percent
Service industries: 34 percent
Per capita income: 12,672
Exports: Fruits, dairy products, textiles, beans, and cotton.
Natural resources: forestry, mining

COAHUILA

GDP in thousands of pesos:
133,950,269
Percent of GDP:
Manufacturing: 11 percent
Commerce: 53 percent
Service industries: 36 percent
Per capita income in pesos: 19,265
Exports: Iron, cotton, grapes, and livestock.
Natural resources: iron ore, lead, silver, zinc, gold, and copper

NUEVO LEÓN

GDP in thousands of pesos:
286,969,565
Percent of GDP:
Manufacturing: 12 percent
Commerce: 51 percent
Service industries: 37 percent
Per capita income in pesos: 24,665
Exports: Glass, glassware, prepared food stuffings, iron, beverages, and chemicals
Natural resources: lead, iron ore, copper

SAN LUIS POTOSÍ

GDP in thousands of pesos:
70,675,085
Percent of GDP:
Manufacturing: 12 percent
Commerce: 53 percent
Service industries: 35 percent
Per capita income in pesos: 10,310
Exports: Minerals, precious metals, chemicals & tropical fruits
Natural resources: agriculture, silver, gold, lead

TAMAULIPAS

GDP in thousands of pesos:
41,998,268
Percent of GDP:
Manufacturing: 9 percent
Commerce: 51 percent
Service industries: 40 percent
Per capita income in pesos: 15,288
Exports: Petrochemicals, fish, and crustaceans.
Natural resources: gold, copper, silver, lead, oil, fish

ZACATECAS

GDP in thousands of pesos:
10,937,468
Percent of GDP:
Manufacturing: 11 percent
Commerce: 55 percent
Service industries: 34 percent
Per capita income: 8,095
Exports: Coffee, fresh fruits, fertilizer, sugar, fish & crustaceans.
Natural resources: gold, copper, silver, lead, zinc

PER CAPITA INCOME = the amount earned in an area divided by the total number of people living in that area
GDP = Gross Domestic Product, the total value of goods and services produced during the year
1 PESO = about $0.10, as of August 2008

Figures from INEGI, the Mexican National Institute of Statistics, based on Mexico's 2000 census.

39

Three canyons meet near the town of Divisadero in the Sierra Tarahumara mountains of Chihuahua. Although the country was colonized by Spain in the 16th century, many of the native peoples, such as the Tarahumara and the Maya, have managed to keep their traditional culture alive.

THE CULTURE

The northern part of Mexico is much closer to the United States geographically and culturally. Much of what goes on in the towns is directed toward the border—the factories, the tourists who come and go. But outside of the cities, in places like the Sierra Tarahumara, the Indians live as they always have.

There are 50 to 70 thousand Tarahumara or *Rarámuri* living in the Copper Canyon in caves, under cliffs, and in small cabins. These people raise corn and beans and some animals. The name Rarámuri means "running people" or "footrunners," and they are known for how fast they run barefoot up the mountains. They are famous for their nonstop, long-distance foot races that may last as long as 72 hours. The phrase they use to describe their running is "foot throwing." A game they like to play is known as *Rarahipa* and involves teams kicking a wooden ball. These people live closely to the earth; they fashion their plows from the limbs of oak trees, and they are skilled in the preparation of more than 200 species of edible plants. They are determined to follow the ancient traditions of their ancestors; for centuries, they have successfully resisted all outside efforts to modernize their way of life.

When you travel from Copper Canyon to a city on the border like Ciudad Juárez, it is almost like traveling through time. The modern border towns have more in common with modern European or American cities than they do with the primitive villages of their own state.

	STATE POPULATION	GROWTH RATE
Chihuahua	3,052,907	2.3%
Coahuila	2,298,070	1.6%
Durango	1,448,661	0.7%
Nuevo León	3,834,141	2.2%
San Luis Potosí	2,299,360	1.4%
Tamaulipas	2,753,222	2.1%
Zacatecas	1,353,610	0.6%

Mexico's ethnic groups:
Indian-Spanish (mestizo): 60 percent
Indian: 30 percent
White: 9 percent
Other: 1 percent

Education: **12 years of education is required from ages 6 through 18. About 94 percent of school-age children are enrolled in school. The literacy rate is 91 percent.**

Mexico's religions:
Roman Catholic: 77 percent
Protestant: 6 percent
Unspecified response: 17 percent

Whether primitive or modern, however, like the rest of Mexico the people of the northern states love to celebrate. They enjoy festivals, fairs, feast days, national holidays, and religious holidays. Every town has its own saint and celebrates on that saint's special day. Local regions also have their own unique celebrations for the harvest of their particular crops. Most of these joyous events involve music, dancing, feasting, and fireworks.

Along with the rest of the nation, northern Mexico celebrates the following holidays:

* *Carnaval*, the Tuesday before the beginning of **Lent**, when people parade through the streets in costumes.
* *Holy Week*, from Palm Sunday to Easter Sunday.

Two Tarahumara girls use a stick to toss a hoop forward as part of a race. They are participating in games and dances in an effort to keep their traditional culture alive.

* *Cinco de Mayo*, May 5, when Mexicans celebrate their victory over France at the battle of Puebla in 1862.
* *Día de la Raza*, October 12 (Columbus Day in the United States), when Mexicans celebrate the mingling of races that makes their nation unique.
* *Día de los Muertos* (Day of the Dead), October 31-November 2, when Mexicans honor their dead with celebrations and feasting.
* *The Feast of the Virgin of Guadalupe*, December 12, when Mexicans honor their patron saint.
* Advent and Christmas, December 16-25, when Mexicans celebrate *Posada*, honoring Mary and Joseph's search for shelter, and then spend Christmas Day as a quiet religious holiday.

Various local cities and regions have their own celebrations as well. In Chihuahua, the Tarahumara people have incorporated the festivals of the Virgin of Guadalupe and *Semana Santa* (Holy Week)

A tourist studies the ruins of a brick building near Copper Canyon in Chihuahua. Tourism has been on the rise in Mexico since the 1970s, when Americans discovered its possibilities as a close, affordable, and beautiful vacation spot.

with their own religious traditions. They celebrate these occasions with elaborate costumes and dancing, honoring the sun, which is their symbol for God, the Mother and Father of their people.

From July 18 to August 3, people of Coahuila flood the streets of Saltillo to celebrate the annual *Feria de Saltillo*. This region was first settled by 400 Tlaxcalteca families, people who were craftsmakers and weavers by trade, and Saltillo's fair celebrates their descendants'

Carnaval stretches over five days, encompassing Mexico's celebration of the traditional holidays before Lent. Festivalgoers dress up and parade for Fat Tuesday and Ash Wednesday, as well as for lesser-known events such as the Day of the Oppressed Husband.

artistry and culture. Colorful woolen *serapes* are a symbol of these people's traditional lifestyle and unique culture.

Every July, Durango celebrates for two weeks. The festival starts July 4, the day of the *Virgen del Refugio*, and continues through July 22, the anniversary of Durango's founding in 1563. The celebration is known throughout Mexico, and people from all over the country come to buy cows, bet on cockfights, and enjoy the food, music, dancing, and rides.

Townsfolk costumed as skeletons carry a coffin through the streets in a mock funeral. Celebrations for the Day of the Dead may appear morbid to outsiders, but they carry a great deal of significance for Mexican participants.

Monterrey, the capital city of Nuevo León, has a very different annual event—a lottery. Every year thousands of hopeful people buy tickets for the national lottery sponsored by Monterrey's Technology Institute. The grand prize is a dream house, designed and built by experts chosen by the Institute. The prize also includes enough money to furnish the house—and an additional sum for upkeep for many years to come.

The people of San Luis Potosí celebrate the last two weeks of August. They flock to the capital city for the *Fiesta Nacional Potosina*. The festival

includes concerts, bullfights, fireworks, and a parade. The celebration of the city's patron saint, San Luis, also falls during this time.

Come May, the city will again celebrate for another 10 days. This time the *Festival de las Artes* will fill the city with music, dance, and theater performances.

The border towns of Tamaulipas are so close to Texas that the United States is a big influence on their culture. Everything tends to cater to the tourists who come in throngs looking for cheap handicrafts and after-dark thrills in the rough bars and cantinas that fill these cities. This area of Mexico is not famous for its food or drink—but many tourists do enjoy the buzz of caffeine they experience when they drink this region's traditional beverage: *café de olla*, a blend of coffee, chocolate, and cinnamon that is brewed slowly in a clay pot.

The people of Zacatecas sometimes celebrate a private **fiesta** called a *callejonada*. A donkey, with gallons of **mescal** on its back, strolls through the alleys and back streets of the capital city. Music and dancing follow along behind—and everyone is welcome to join the party.

The Rancho de las Golondrinas is now a living history museum. In the early 1700s, however, it was an important stop along the famous Camino Real, or Royal Road, from Mexico City to Santa Fe, New Mexico.

CITIES AND COMMUNITIES

Many of Mexico's most modern, wealthy, and industrialized cities lie opposite the United States along the northern border. Some Mexicans feel that the United States dominates Mexico, intruding where it doesn't belong. Many believe that U.S. businesses take advantage of the cheap labor of the Mexican workers.

In these northern cities are the *maquiladoras*—the factories that are often owned by companies from the United States. Here too people regularly go back and forth over the border into the United States, sometimes working in one country and living in the other. Perhaps more than in any other part of Mexico, people in the northern states' cities feel related to the United States. Indeed, they often have relations across the border.

Chihuahua City, with nearly a million people, is the 12th-largest city in Mexico and one of its most industrialized. Timber and mining concerns, as well as *maquiladoras*, are based in Chihuahua, although the dog that takes its name from the city is rarely seen.

Originally settled by silver miners at the start of the 18th century, Chihuahua has served as a refuge for many political figures. Miguel Hidalgo fled here during the War of Independence, and here Benito Juárez lived during the Revolution. The city's most famous resident and greatest hero was the outlaw Pancho Villa. In the Museum of the Revolution you can see the car he was driving when he was assassinated in 1923. The car is just as he last saw it, bullet holes and all.

Since NAFTA, Ciudad Juárez has become a thriving city. Once known as Paso del Norte, Juárez marks the spot where Don Juan de Oñate crossed the Río Grande. This occurred 60 years after the arrival of Cortés and 40 years before the Pilgrims came to Plymouth Rock. In 1668 Father García de San Francisco founded the Mission of Our Lady of Guadalupe where mass is still said daily. Juárez served as an important way station along the Camino Real (Royal Road), and the cattle drivers would stop here to water their herds on the way to Texas. Some of its most famous inhabitants have included outlaws like Billy the Kid, John Wesley Hardin, and Pancho Villa. In 1856, Benito Juárez established his government here and the city was renamed in his honor.

The state of Chihuahua contains people as diverse as the land itself. In the 1920s, *Mennonites* from the United States were attracted here by the rich pastures, and today they still maintain their communities in Chihuahua's agricultural areas. Like the Mennonites, the Tarahumara people live in isolation from the rest of the world, but their ancient native culture is far different. The Tarahumara sell their crafts in Chihuahua's cities, and then retreat to their simple lifestyle in Chihuahua's Sierra Madres.

Two Mennonite men lean against a wall in a Mennonite settlement in Mexico, while a young boy scans the surrounding area. Mennonites from the United States moved into Mexico during the early 20th century, attracted by the fertile land as well as the opportunity to raise their families isolated from other cultures.

Saltillo, capital of Coahuila and the 21st largest city in Mexico, boasts walnut trees, vineyards, and pleasant temperatures. Once a cattle farming town, Saltillo's fresh climate has made it a pleasant stopping place. Saltillo is known for its colorful serapes.

Francisco de Ibarra founded the city of Durango in 1564 and named it after his hometown in Spain. In 1616 Durango was the scene of a bloody Indian rebellion where 15,000 people died. Today, much of Durango's wealth comes out of one of the largest iron deposits in the world, under the mountain Cerro de Mercado. You may have seen the city of Durango a thousand times in the Western movies that were filmed here. Such film stars as John Wayne and Paul Newman have come here to star in Westerns that were filmed in the spectacular desert scenery.

A poster advertising a bullfight in Monterrey is displayed on a public wall. Many Mexicans are passionate about keeping their culture alive through customs and traditions.

Monterrey, the capital city and the third largest city in Mexico, is called the "Pittsburgh of Mexico" because of the many mills that convert the country's iron and coal reserves into steel. Monterrey is the major center of the Mexican steel industry—and it is also known for its 20 colleges. *Fortune* magazine voted Monterrey the best city in Latin America for business. With air conditioning, modern buildings, and shopping malls, it would be hard to distinguish Monterrey from any large city in the United States. Eighty-five percent of Nuevo León's population lives here in this modern city. Three thousand trucks pass through daily on their way to and from Texas.

Despite Monterrey's industrial wealth, the city has a reputation throughout Mexico as being a place where stingy people live. In fact,

This statue of Father Miguel Hidalgo stands in the middle of a village plaza. Following Mexico's Independence Day, this statue will be adorned with red, white, and green flowers to acknowledge Hidalgo's influence in the fight for a free Mexico.

they're thought to be so tight-fisted that if you want to order a glass of ice water in a Mexican restaurant, just ask for "A Monterrey on the rocks."

In the 17th century, the city of San Luis Potosí, the state's present-day capital, was the capital of Northern New Spain. It was also home to Juárez, and here he signed the death sentence of the Emperor Maximilian. Today San Luis Potosí calls itself Ciudad de los Jardines, the city of gardens, because of its many parks. Overall, though, this is an industrial city with factories, and a few well-preserved old buildings.

Matamoros, directly across the border from Brownsville, Texas, boasts the Museum of Corn as well as a fort left from the Mexican-American War. Matamoros also has a significant Jewish population, since Jewish families from the center of Mexico settled here in the early 20th century to avoid religious persecution. The first *maquiladora* in Mexico was built here, and

Benito Pablo Juárez was born to Zapotec Indian parents in Oaxaca. He went on to twice be elected president of his country. His main goal was to apply some degree of reform to the tumultuous government of Mexico.

today there are 120 of these factories. With 490,000 residents, Matamoros is the 15th-largest city in Mexico. Nuevo Laredo is located in the state of Tamaulipas on the border of Mexico and the United States. This city was founded in 1755 when Laredo, Texas, became part of the United States. At that time, some Mexican people crossed to the south of the Río Grande to establish a "new" Laredo, because they wanted to remain Mexicans. Between 1950 and 1995, Nuevo Laredo has grown nearly five times over. Currently, it has a population of slightly over 350,000, and it has been projected to grow to over 400,000 residents in the next few years.

Tampico, a bustling port town in Tamaulipas, has a population of 313,400 and is the 44th-largest city in the country. The largest city in

Tamaulipas, Tampico was first settled by Huastec Indians and then by the Aztecs. Today, Tampico is still famous for an incident between Mexico and the United States that occurred in 1914. The United States captured the port, helping the rebels overthrow President Huerta.

The city of Zacatecas, the capital of the state, winds like a maze built in between and on top of steep hills. The buildings at the center of town are built from a rosy sandstone, which makes the city seem brightly pink. It was once a prosperous silver town, and it still supplies 34 percent of Mexico's silver. The beautiful Templo de Santo Domingo, filled with ornate golden decoration, was built between 1730 and 1760; it represents of a style of architecture for which Mexico is famous— Churrigueresque. Named for José Churriguera, a Spanish architect, this style is extravagant and fancy; it combined elements of both Spanish and native Mexican architecture.

As you travel from one of these cities to the next, it is impossible not to be struck by the history that lives in each of them. The past and present lie in layers, from modern skyscrapers to ancient churches. The echoes of **Nahuatl**, Spanish, and English voices come together in an exciting symphony.

Mexico's cities' greatest strength has always come from their people—their unique culture, their creativity, and their faith. The problems handed down from past centuries are still visible in these cities' poverty—but as the Mexican people work with a new administration, who knows how the northern states will grow in the century to come?

CHRONOLOGY

150 B.C.	Teotihuacán is built.
A.D. 750	Teotihuacán is abandoned.
300–900	Peak cultural growth of the Maya.
	Aztecs begin to conquer other tribes for control of Mexico.
1325	Aztecs build Tenochtitlán.
1521	Spanish take control of Mexico.
1810	Father Miguel Hidalgo calls for Mexico's independence from Spain.
1821	Mexico wins its independence.
1862	France invades Mexico.
1867	Benito Juárez triumphs over the French, executes the Emperor Maximilian, and resumes his presidency.
1876	Porfirio Díaz begins his period of dictatorship.
1910–1921	The Mexican Revolution.
1968	Mexico hosts the Summer Olympic Games, and violence breaks out during a student protest.
2000	Vicente Fox becomes president.
2004	Monterrey hosts the Summit of the Americas, in which the leaders of 34 Western Hemisphere democracies meet to discuss political issues.
2006	65 workers are killed in an explosion at a Coahuila coal mine; Felipe Calderón is elected president of Mexico.
2008	Despite the efforts of Mexican law enforcement agencies, drug-related gang violence remains a major problem in the northern states near the U.S. border.

56

FOR MORE INFORMATION

CHIHUAHUA

Government of Chihuahua
http://www.chihuahua.gob.mx

State Tourism Office
Palacio de Gobierno
Planta Baja
Aldama y Vicente Guerrero
Col. Centro
Chihuahua, Chih.
Tel: (614) 410-10-77
E-mail: cturismo@chihuahua.gob.mx

COAHUILA

Government of Coahuila
http://www.coahuila.gob.mx

State Tourism Office
Av. Universidad
No. 205, Col. Republica Poniente
25280 Saltillo, Coah.
Tel: (844) 416-4880
Fax: (844) 439-2747

DURANGO

Government of Durango
http://www.durango.gob.mx

State Tourism Office
Calle Florida No. 1106, Piso Barrio
El Calvario, Zona Centro
CP 34000
Durango, Dgo.
Tel: (618) 811-2139/1107
Fax: (618) 811-9677
E-mail: turismo@durango.gob.mx

NUEVO LEÓN

Government of Nuevo León
http://www.nuevoleon.gob.mx

State Tourism Office
Antiguo Palacio Federal
Washington ote 648, First Floor
Centro
CP64000 Monterrey, N.L.
Tel: (81) 2020-6789

FOR MORE INFORMATION

SAN LUIS POTOSÍ

Government of San Luis Potosí
http://www.slp.gob.mx

State Tourism Office
Álvaro Obregón No. 520
Zona Central
CP 78000 San Luis Potosí, S.L.P.
Tel: (444) 812-9906
E-mail: turisslp@prodigy.net.mx

ZACATECAS

Government of Zacatecas
http://www.zacatecas.gob.mx

State Tourism Office
Av. Hidalgo No. 403, Segundo Piso
Col. Centro
CP 98000 Zacatecas, Zac.
Tel: (492) 924-0552
Fax: (492) 924-0393

TAMAULIPAS

Government of Tamaulipas
http://www.tamaulipas.gob.mx

State Tourism Office
Calle 9 Hernán Cortés No. 136
Col. Pedro Sosa, Edif. El Peñón,
CP 87120 Cd. Victoria, Tamps.
Tel: (834) 315-6248/6249/6136/6137
    ext. 201

THINGS TO DO AND SEE

CHIHUAHUA

Copper Canyon

Cerocahui's Tarahumar dances and Jesuit mission

Sangre de Cristo gold mines

COAHUILA

La Cascada de Caballo (Horsetail Falls), a dramatic waterfall

Saltillo's cultural center

DURANGO

Regional Museum of Durango, containing fossils and mummies

The city of Durango's Palacio de Gobierno, a baroque palace that houses two of
   Mexico's great 20th-century murals, one by Francisco Montoya and the other
   by Ernesto Flores Esquivel

NUEVO LEÓN

Parque de los Niños Heroes (Park of the Child Heroes), which also contains
   several museums

SAN LUIS POTOSÍ

Santa María del Río, a village famous for its handcrafted silk and cotton shawls.
   These techniques originated in Asia centuries ago, were passed to Spain during
   the Moors' invasion, and then were brought to Mexico by the conquistadors.

Real de Catorce, a ghost town

TAMAULIPAS

The beaches of Tampico

El Cielo Nature Preserve

ZACATECAS

The aqueduct of the city of Zacatecas

Cerro de la Bufa (Hill of the Wineskin), a hill that allows a magnificent view of
   the surrounding landscape; a museum, chapel, and cemetery are also on the hill

Eden Mine, which operated from the 1500s until 1964

59

FURTHER READING

Chávez, Alicia Hernández. *Mexico: A Brief History*. Berkeley: University of California Press, 2006.

Coe, Michael D., and Rex Koontz. *Mexico: From the Olmecs to the Aztecs*. New York: Thames and Hudson, 2008.

Hamnet, Brian R. *A Concise History of Mexico*. New York: Cambridge University Press, 2006.

Joseph, Gilbert M., editor. *The Mexico Reader: History, Culture, Politics*. Durham, N.C.: Duke University Press, 2002.

Levy, Daniel C., and Kathleen Bruhn. *Mexico: The Struggle for Democratic Development*. Berkeley: University of California Press, 2006.

Mayor, Guy. *Mexico: A Quick Guide to Customs and Etiquette*. New York: Kuperard, 2006.

INTERNET RESOURCES

INEGI (Geographic, Demographic, and Economic Information of Mexico)
http://www.inegi.gob.mx/diffusion/ingles/portadai.html

Mesoweb
http://www.mesoweb.com/welcome.html#externalresources

Mexico for Kids
http://www.elbalero.gob.mx/index_kids.html

Mexico Channel
http://www.mexicochannel.net

GLOSSARY

Aqueducts	Bridge-like structures that carry water pipes.
Cabinet	An advisory council to the head of a government.
Cisterns	An underground tank for storing drinking water.
Conquistadors	Spanish conquerors of the New World.
Exported	Shipped goods or services out of a country.
Fiesta	Spanish party or celebration.
Haciendas	Large Mexican ranches.
Immunities	The body's abilities to resist certain diseases.
Imported	Brought goods or services into a country.
Interest rates	The percent at which loans and savings increase.
Irrigated	Brought water to the land by artificial means.
Lent	The six weeks before Easter, a time of fasting and repentance.
Jesuit	A member of the Roman Catholic Society of Jesus, founded by St. Ignatius Loyola in 1534 and devoted to missionary and educational work.
Mennonites	Members of a Protestant religious group who believe in pacifism and sometime isolate themselves from the influences of modern society.
Mescal	A colorless Mexican liquor distilled from the leaves of maguey plants.
Migrate	To move from one region to another.
Nahuatl	The ancient language spoken by the Aztecs; still spoken by many modern Mexicans.
Petition	A formal written request, usually signed by many people.
Plateau	High, level land.
Serapes	Colorful woolen shawls worn by Mexican men.
Vaqueros	Mexican cowboys.

INDEX

PICTURE CREDITS

CONTRIBUTORS

Roger E. Hernández is the most widely syndicated columnist writing on Hispanic issues in the United States. His weekly column, distributed by King Features, appears in some 40 newspapers across the country, including the *Washington Post*, *Los Angeles Daily News*, *Dallas Morning News*, *Arizona Republic*, *Rocky Mountain News* in Denver, *El Paso Times*, and *Hartford Courant*. He is also the author of *Cubans in America*, an illustrated history of the Cuban presence in what is now the United States, from the early colonists in 16th-century Florida to today's Castro-era exiles. The book was designed to accompany a PBS documentary of the same title.

Hernández's articles and essays have been published in the *New York Times*, *New Jersey Monthly*, *Reader's Digest*, and *Vista Magazine*; he is a frequent guest on television and radio political talk shows, and often travels the country to lecture on his topic of expertise. Currently, he is teaching journalism and English composition at the New Jersey Institute of Technology in Newark, where he holds the position of writer-in-residence. He is also a member of the adjunct faculty at Rutgers University.

Hernández left Cuba with his parents at the age of nine. After living in Spain for a year, the family settled in Union City, New Jersey, where Hernández grew up. He attended Rutgers University, where he earned a BA in Journalism in 1977; after graduation, he worked in television news before moving to print journalism in 1983. He lives with his wife and two children in Upper Montclair, New Jersey.

AUTHOR

Deirdre Day-MacLeod is a freelance writer. She lives in Montclair, New Jersey. She is also the author of *The States of Central Mexico*.